Hon. A. C. Barstow;
With sincere regards of
Compiler.

# HOMAGE

OF

EMINENT PERSONS

TO

# THE BOOK.

"There is but one book—THE BIBLE."

COMPILED BY

SAMUEL W. BAILEY.

---

" How precious is the Book divine,
  By inspiration given!
Bright as a lamp its doctrines shine,
  To guide our souls to heaven."

---

NEW YORK.
1871.

Rand, Avery, & Frye,
Stereotypers and Printers,
3 Cornhill, Boston.

# PROLOGUE.

---

THEY who have truly begun to learn the value of the Bible need few incentives to study it further. Whoever has had a taste of honey, or has been cheered by genial sunlight, will not refuse the one for bitter and poisonous weeds, nor prefer the darkness and chilly damps of a prison to the other. But many, unhappily, have never gained a relish for the wondrous truths of the Bible, nor been charmed by its literary beauties. It would befit a philosopher to account for such lack of susceptibility. A kindlier service is here rendered.

Wise men credit the testimony of explorers and discoverers, as they are believed to be sagacious, upright, and truthful. An imposing array of witnesses, renowned for wisdom and genius, for patriotism and philanthropy, here testify to the same point, — a point to which they were qualified to speak. The statesman and the jurist, the poet and the orator, the philosopher, moralist, and the divine, successively assert and justify the claims of the Sacred Oracles to be reverently and faithfully studied. From such a number and variety of authors, a large volume of testimony like this might be gathered; but it is here deemed unwise to overtask the patience of the most moderate reader.

It is but frank, however, to say, that, while minds mature and cultivated may derive advantage from this compilation, it is chiefly designed for persons whose tastes, opinions, and habits are still pliant and forming. And since the known sentiments and opinions of virtuous and intelligent parents rightfully sway their children, ought not the worth and wisdom of those distinguished representatives of different periods and countries to clothe their earnest words, here recorded, with more than parental authority? Be it that the word is unpleasing and unpopular:

there is still that *authority* pertaining to integrity of character, to soundness of judgment, to largeness of observation and experience, and to arguments brief, but terse and forcible, which none may wisely disregard.

If this little book shall beget an increased interest in the Bible, and a greater practical reverence for its teachings; if it shall prevail to *silence cavillers*, or to fortify its readers against their malign sophistries and quibbles; and if it shall prove to be an antidote, however feeble, to the present excessive taste for *works of fiction*, by fostering an opposite one for *wholesome and vital truths*, — it will achieve ends both needful and benign.

# CONTENTS.

## *PART I.*



## *PART II.*



## *PART III.*

# INDEX.

# PART I.

## HOMAGE OF EMINENT PERSONS IN WORDS MISCELLANEOUS.

### I.

By Rev. HENRY WARD BEECHER.

*Dispense with the Bible?*

MANY will say, "I can find God without the help of the Bible or church or minister." Very well. Do so if you can. The ferry company would feel no jealousy of a man who should prefer to swim to New York. Let him do so if he is able, and we will talk about it on the other shore; but, probably, trying to swim would be the thing that would bring him quickest to the boat. So God would have no jealousy of a man's going to heaven without the aid of the Bible or church or minister; but let him try to do so, and it will be the surest way to bring him back to them for assistance.

"Be thou my star in reason's night;
Be thou my rock in danger's fright;
Be thou my guide mid passion's way;
My moon by night, my sun by day."

DEAN MILMAN TO HIS BIBLE.

## II.

By Hon. JOHN ADAMS, second President of the United States. — 1735–1826.

*The Bible the best of Books.**

I HAVE examined all, as well as my narrow sphere, my straitened means, and my busy life, would allow me; and the result is, that the Bible is the best book in the world. It contains more of my little philosophy than all the libraries I have seen; and such parts of it as I cannot reconcile to my little philosophy, I postpone for future investigation.

* From a Letter to Thomas Jefferson, dated December, 1813.

*From his Diary.*

Suppose a nation in some distant region should take the Bible for their only law-book, and every member should regulate his conduct by the precepts there exhibited. Every member would be obliged, in conscience, to temperance and frugality and industry, to justice and kindness and charity towards his fellow-men, and to piety, love, and reverence towards Almighty God. In this commonwealth, no man would impair his health by gluttony, drunkenness, or lust: no man would sacrifice his most precious time to cards, or any other trifling or mean amusement; no man would steal or lie, or in any way defraud his neighbor, but would live in peace and good will with all men; no man would blaspheme his Maker, or profane his worship; but a rational and manly, a sincere and unaffected, piety and devotion would reign in all hearts.

## III.

By JOHN SELDEN, the Oriental Scholar.—1584–1654.

*The Same.*

THOUGH I have been very laborious in my literary inquiries, and have possessed myself of a great number of valuable books and manuscripts upon all ancient subjects, yet I can rest the happiness of my soul on none of them except the Holy Scriptures.

## IV.

By Rev. EDWARD PAYSON, D.D.—1783–1827.

*The Best Companionships in the Bible.*

BY opening this volume we may at any time walk in the garden of Eden with Adam, sit in the ark with Noah, share the hospitality or witness the faith of Abraham, ascend the mount of God with Moses, unite in the secret devotions of David, or listen to the eloquent and impassioned address of Paul. Nay, more: we may here converse with Him who spake as never man spake, participate with the just made perfect in the employment and happiness of heaven, and enjoy sweet communion with the Father of our spirits through his Son Jesus Christ. Such is the society to which the Scriptures introduce us, such the examples which they present to our imitation.

## V.

By J. W. V. GOETHE, the Poet. — 1740–1832.

*The Bible as a Guide.*

IT is a belief in the Bible, the fruits of deep meditation, which has served me as the guide of my moral and literary life. I have found it a capital safely invested, and richly productive of interest.

## VI.

By HENRY VAUGHAN, the Poet. — 1621–1695.

O BOOK! life's guard!
Thou wert the first put in my hand,
When yet I could not understand;
And daily didst my young eyes lead
To letters, till I learnt to read.

But as rash youths, when once grown strong,
Flee from their nurses to the throng,
Where they new consorts choose, and stick
To those till either hurt or sick;
So, with that first light gained from thee,
Ran I in chase of vanity;
Cried "dross" for gold; and never thought
My first cheap book had all I sought.

## VII.

By Hon. JOHN QUINCY ADAMS to a Literary Society of Young Men.* — 1767–1848.

*Advice as to a Course of General Reading.*

THE first and almost the only book deserving universal attention is the Bible; and, in recommending that, I fear that some of you will think I am performing a superfluous, and others a very unnecessary office: yet such is my deliberate opinion. The Bible is the book of all others, to be read at all ages, and in all conditions of human life; not to be read once

* From a letter addressed by Hon. John Quincy Adams to a literary society of young men in Baltimore, who had sought his advice as to a course of general reading. It is dated "Washington, June 22, 1838."

or twice or thrice through, and then laid aside, but to be read in small portions of one or two chapters every day, and never to be intermitted unless by some overruling necessity.

I speak as a man of the world to men of the world; and I say to you, *Search the Scriptures!* If ever you tire of them in seeking a rule of faith and a standard of morals, search them as records of history. The Bible contains the only authentic introduction to the history of the world. It is a book which neither the most ignorant and weakest, nor the most learned and intelligent mind can read without improvement.

*Advice to his Son.*

For pathos of narrative; for the selections of incidents that go directly to the heart; for the picturesque of character and manner; the selection of circumstances that mark the individuality of persons; for copiousness, grandeur, and sublimity of imagery; for unanswerable cogency and closeness of reasoning; and for irresistible force of persuasion,—no book in the world deserves to be so unceasingly studied, and so profoundly meditated upon, as the Bible.

I advise you, my son, in whatever you read, and most of all in reading the Bible, always to read it with reference to some particular train of observation or reflection. In these letters, I have suggested to you four general ones. Considering the Scriptures as divine revelations; as historic records; as containing a system of morals; and as literary compositions, — I have myself, for many years, made it a practice to read through the Bible once every year. My custom is to read four or five chapters every morning, immediately after rising from my bed. It employs about an hour of my time, and seems to be the most suitable manner of beginning the day

## VIII.

### By Edmund Burke. — 1730–1797.

*The Bible a Source of Happiness.*

I HAVE been educated as a Protestant of the Church of England, by a *dissenter*, who was an honor to his sect, though that sect was considered one of the purest. Under his eye, I have read the Bible morning, noon, and night, and have ever since been the happier and better man for such reading.

## IX.

By Sir MATTHEW HALE, Chief Justice of England. — Born 1609; died 1676.

*Advice to his Children.*

EVERY morning, read seriously and reverently a portion of the Holy Scriptures, and acquaint yourselves with the history and doctrine thereof. It is a book full of light and wisdom, will make you wise to eternal life, and furnish you with directions and principles to guide and order your life safely and prudently. There is no book like the Bible for excellent learning, wisdom, and use.

## X.

Dying words of WILLIAM WILBERFORCE. — 1759–1833.

*The Bible should be first and chiefly read.*

READ the Bible, read the Bible! Let no religious book take its place. Through all my perplexities and distresses, I seldom read any other book, and I as rarely felt the want of any other. It has been my hourly study; and all my knowledge of the doctrines, and all my acquaintance with the experience and realities of religion, have been chiefly derived from the Bible. I think that religious people do not read the Bible enough. Books about religion may be useful; but they will not do instead of the simple truth of the Bible.

## XI.

By John Wilson ("Christopher North"), Late Professor of Moral Philosophy in the University of Edinburgh.—1785–1854.

*Benefits of Early Familiarity with the Bible.*

HE who is so familiar with his Bible, that each chapter, open it where he will, teems with household words, may draw thence the theme of many a pleasant and pathetic song. For is not all human nature and all human life shadowed forth in those pages? But the heart, to sing well from the Bible, must be imbued with religious feelings, as a flower is alternately with dew and sunshine. The study of *The Book* must have begun in the simplicity of childhood, when it was felt to be indeed divine, and carried on through all those silent intervals in which the soul of manhood is restored, during the din of life, to the purity and peace of its early being. The Bible to such must be a port, even as the sky, with its sun, moon, and stars; its boundless blue, with all its cloud-mysteries; its peace deeper than the grave, because of realms beyond the grave; its tumult louder than that of life, because heard altogether in all the elements. He who begins the study of the Bible late in life must, indeed, devote himself to it night and day, and with a humble and contrite heart, as well as an awakened and soaring spirit, ere he can hope to feel what he understands, or to understand what he feels; thoughts and feelings breathing in upon him, as if from a region hanging in its mystery between heaven and earth.

## XII.

By Rev. JOHN FLAVEL. — 1627–1691.

*Bible Teachings.*

THE Scriptures teach us the best way of *living*, the *noblest way of suffering*, and the *most comfortable way of dying*.

## XIII.

By Rev. JAMES HAMILTON. — Died 1868.

*The Bible adapted to all.*

IN His wisdom and goodness, the Most High has judged far better for our world; and using the agency of forty authors, transfusing through the peculiar tastes and temperaments of so many individuals — and these "men of like passions with ourselves" — the self-same truths, the Spirit of God has secured for the Bible universal adaptation. For the pensive, there is the dirge of Jeremiah and the cloud-shadowed drama of Job; for the sanguine and hopeful, there sounds the blithe voice, and there beats the warm pulse, of old Galilean Peter; and for the calm, the contemplative, the peacefully loving, there spreads, like a molten melody or an abysmal joy, the page — sunny, ecstatic, boundless — of John the divine. The most homely may find the matter-of-fact, the unvarnished wisdom, and plain sense, which is the chosen aliment of their sturdy understandings, in James's blunt reasonings; and the most heroic can ask no higher standard, no loftier feats, no consecration more intense, no spirituality more ethereal, than they will find in the Pauline Epistles. Those who love the sparkling aphorism and the sagacious paradox are provided with food convenient in the Proverbs; and for those whose poetic fancy craves a banquet more sublime, there is the dew of Hermon and Bozrah's red wine, the tender freshness of pastoral hymns, and the purple tumult of triumphal psalms.

## XIV.

By Chancellor JAMES KENT.— 1763-1847.

*The same.*

THE Bible is equally adapted to the wants and infirmities of every human being. It is the vehicle of the most awful truths, and which are at the same time of universal application, and accompanied by the most efficacious sanctions. No other book ever addressed itself so authoritatively and so pathetically to the judgment and moral sense of mankind. It contains the most sublime and fearful displays of the attributes of that perfect Being who inhabiteth eternity, and pervades and governs the universe. It brings life and immortality to light, which, until the publication of the gospel, were hidden from the scrutiny of ages. Its doctrines, its discoveries, its code of morals, and its means of grace, are not only overwhelming evidence of its divine origin, but they confound the pretensions of all other systems, by showing the narrow range and feeble efforts of human reason, even when under the sway of the most exalted understanding, and enlightened by the accumulated treasures of science and learning.

## XV.

### By Prof. Gaussen, of Geneva.

*The same.*

As a skilful musician, called to execute alone some masterpiece, puts his lips by turns to the mournful flute, the shepherd's reed, the mirthful pipe, and the war-trumpet; so the Almighty God, to sound in our ears his eternal Word, has selected from of old the instruments best suited to receive successively the breath of his Spirit. Thus we have, in God's great anthem of revelation, the sublime simplicity of John, the argumentative, elliptical, soul-stirring energy of Paul, the fervor and solemnity of Peter, the poetic grandeur of Isaiah, the lyric moods of David, the ingenuous and majestic narratives of Moses, the sententious and royal wisdom of Solomon. Yes: it was all this, — it was Peter, Isaiah, Matthew, John, or Moses; but it was God.

## XVI.

By GREGORY the Great. — Elected Pope 1049. Died 1085.

*The same.*

A STREAM where alike the elephant may swim, and the lamb may wade.

## XVII.

By Rev. RICHARD CECIL. — 1748–1810.

*The Bible a Mirror of Human Character and of the Inward Life.*

PRINCIPLE is to be distinguished from prejudice. The man who should endeavor to weaken my belief of the truth of the Bible, and of the fair deductions from it of the leading doctrines of religion, under the notion of their being prejudices, should be regarded by me as an assassin. He stabs me in my deepest hopes; he robs me of my solid happiness; and he has no equivalent to offer. This species of evidence of the truth and value of Scripture is within the reach of all men. It is my strongest. It assures me, as fully as a voice could from heaven, that my principles are not prejudices. I see in the Bible *my heart and the world painted to the life;* and I see just that provision made which is competent to the highest ends and effects on this heart and this world.

> "Thy Word, a wondrous guiding star,
> On pilgrim hearts doth rise;
> Leads to their Lord who dwell afar,
> And makes the simple wise.
> Let not its light
> E'er sink in night,
> But still in every spirit shine,
> That none may miss this light divine."

LYRA GERMANICA.

## XVIII.

By GEORGE HORNE, D.D., Bishop of Norwich.
1730–1792.

*Bible Truths divinely transforming.*

THE Scriptures are wonderful, with respect to the matter which they contain, the manner in which they are written, and the effects which they produce. They contain the sublimest truths, many of which are veiled under external ceremonies and figurative descriptions. When they are properly opened and enforced, they terrify and humble, they convert and transform, they console and strengthen. Who but must delight to study and to observe these testimonies of the will and the wisdom, the love and the power, of God most high! While we have these holy writings, let us not waste our time, misemploy our thoughts, and prostitute our admiration, by doting on human follies, and wondering at human trifles.

## XIX.

### By JOHN LOCKE, the Philosopher. — 1632–1704.

*The Bible a Mysterious Source of Repose.*

I GRATEFULLY receive and rejoice in the light of revelation, which has set me at rest in many things, the manner whereof my poor reason can by no means make out to me.

## XX.

By St. CHRYSOSTOM, Archbishop of Constantinople. — 354–407.

*The Truths of the Bible the Soul's best Food.*

YEA, rather, the reading of the divine Scriptures is not a meadow only, but a paradise; for the flowers here have not a mere fragrance only, but fruit too, capable of nourishing the soul. Assuredly, then, we ought not hastily to pass by even those sentences of Scripture which are thought to be plain; for these also have proceeded from the grace of the Spirit: but this grace is never small nor mean, but great and admirable, and worthy the munificence of the giver; for pearls, too, take their price, not from the size of the substance, but from the beauty of it. Even so is it with the reading of the divine Scriptures; for worldly instruction rolls forth its trifles in abundance, and deluges its hearers with a torrent of vain babblings, but dismisses them empty-handed, and without having gathered any profit, great or small.

## XXI.

### By Rev. John Foster.— 1770–1843.

*The Gospel adapted alike to Minds, however gifted or grovelling.*

IT is the beneficent distinction of the gospel, that, notwithstanding it is of a magnitude to interest and to surpass angelic iuvestigation (and therefore assuredly to pour contempt on the pride of human intelligence that rejects it for its meanness), it is yet most expressly sent to the class which philosophers have always despised. And a good man feels it a cause of grateful joy, that a communication has come from heaven, adapted to effect the happiness of multitudes, in spite of natural debility or neglected education.

## XXII.

*The Bible superior to all other Books.* — Edwards.

IN what other writings can we descry those excellences which we find in the Bible? None of them are equal to it in antiquity; for the first penman of the sacred Scripture hath the start of all philosophers, poets, and historians, and is absolutely the ancientest writer extant in the world. No writings are equal to those of the Bible, if we mention only the stock of human learning contained in them. Here linguists and philologists may find that which is to be found nowhere. Here rhetoricians and orators may be entertained with a more lofty eloquence, with a choicer composure of words, and with a greater variety of style, than any other writers can afford them. Here is a book where more is understood than expressed; where words are few, but the sense is full and redundant. No books equal this in authority, because it is the Word of God himself, and dictated by an unerring Spirit. It excels other writings in the excellency of its matter, which is the highest, noblest, and worthiest, and of the greatest concern to mankind. Lastly, the Scriptures transcend all other writings in their power and efficacy.

## XXIII.

### From Massillon, Bishop of Clermont.—1663–1742.

*The Superiority of Biblical History.*

IN the histories which have been left us by men, we see nothing but the agency of man. They are men who obtain the victories, who take towns, who subdue kingdoms, who dethrone sovereigns, to elevate themselves to the supreme power. God appears in no part: men are the sole actors of all these things. But, in the history of the Holy Books, it is God alone who performs the whole. God alone causeth kings to reign, placeth them upon their thrones, or deposeth them again. It is God alone who opposeth the enemy, who sacks towns, who disposeth of kingdoms and empires, who giveth peace or exciteth war. God alone appeareth in sacred history: it is He, if I may so speak, who is the sole hero. The kings and conquerors of the earth appear but as the ministers of His will. In short, these divine books unfold the ways of Providence. God, who conceals Himself in the other events recorded in our histories, seems to reveal Himself in these; and it is in this book alone that we ought to learn to read the other histories which men have left us.

## XXIV.

By SAMUEL HAYES. — Born 1760.

The sacred page
With calm attention scan. If on thy soul,
As thou dost read, a ray of purer light
Break in, oh! check it not: give it full scope.
Admitted, it will break the clouds which long
Have dimmed thy sight, and lead thee, till at last
Convictions, like the sun's meridian beams,
Illuminate thy mind.

## XXV.

By Hon. ROBERT BOYLE, the Christian Philosopher. — 1626 - 1691.

*The Bible most Forcibly Instructive and Impressively Grand.*

THE Bible is indeed amongst books what the diamond is amongst stones, — the preciousest and the sparklingest; the most apt to scatter light, and yet the solidest and the most proper to make impressions. . . And as the Word of God is termed a light, so hath it this property of what it is called, that both the plainest rustics may, if they will not wilfully shut their eyes, by the benefit of its light, direct their steps, and the deepest philosophers may be exercised with its abstruser mysteries. For thus, in the Scripture, the ignorant may learn all requisite knowledge, and the most knowing may learn to discern their ignorance.

The books of Scripture illustrate and expound each other: as, in the mariner's compass, the needle's extremity, though it seem to point purposely at the north, doth yet at the same time discover both east and west, as distant as they are from it and from each other; so do some texts of Scripture guide us to the intelligence of others, from which they are widely distant in the Bible, and seem so in the sense.

I use the Scripture, not as an arsenal to be resorted to only for arms and weapons to defend this party, or to defeat its enemies, but as a matchless temple, where I delight to be to contemplate the beauty, the symmetry, and the magnificence of the structure, and to increase my awe and to excite my devotion to the Deity there preached and adored.

## XXVI.

By ABRAHAM COWLEY, the Poet.
1618–1667.

*The Bible the best Exemplifier and Source of Poetry.*

ALL the books of the Bible are either already most admirable and exalted pieces of poesy, or are the best materials in the world for it. Amongst all holy and consecrated things which the Devil ever stole and alienated from the service of the Deity, as altars, temples, sacrifices, prayers, and the like, there is none that he so universally and so long usurped as poetry. It is time to recover it out of the tyrant's hands, and to restore it to the kingdom of God, who is the father of it. It is time to baptize it in Jordan; for it will never become clean by bathing in the water of Damascus.

When I consider how many bright and magnificent subjects the Holy Scripture affords and proffers, as it were, to poesy, in the wise managing and illustrating whereof the glory of God Almighty might be joined with the singular utility and noblest delight of mankind, it is not without grief and indignation that I behold that divine science employing all her inexhaustable riches of wit and eloquence, either in the wicked and beggarly flattery of great persons, or the unmanly idolizing of foolish women.

## XXVII.

### By Alexander Pope. — 1688–1744.

*The Bible Inimitable.*

THE pure and noble, the graceful and dignified simplicity of language, is nowhere in such perfection as in the Scriptures and Homer. The whole Book of Job, with regard to simplicity of thought and morality, exceeds, beyond all comparison, the most noble parts of Homer.

## XXVIII.

### By Robert Hall, the Eloquent Divine. — 1764–1831.

*The Literary Attractions of the Bible.*

THERE is something in the spirit and diction of the Bible which is found peculiarly adapted to arrest the attention of the plainest and most uncultivated minds. The simple structure of its sentences, combined with a lofty spirit of poetry: its familiar allusion to the scenes of Nature and the transactions of common life; the delightful intermixture of narration with the doctrinal and preceptive parts; and the profusion of miraculous facts, which convert it into a sort of enchanted ground; its constant advertence to the Deity, whose perfections it renders almost visible and palpable, — unite in bestowing upon it an interest which attaches to no other performance, and which, after assiduous and repeated perusal, invests it with much of the charm of novelty, like the great orb of day, at which we are wont to gaze with unabated astonishment from infancy to old age. What other book besides the Bible could be heard in public assemblies from year to year with an attention that never tires, and an interest that never cloys?

## XXIX.

By Rev. JAMES HAMILTON. — Died 1868.

*The same.*

BUT, in giving that Bible, its divine Author had regard to the mind of man. He knew that man has more curiosity than piety, more taste than sanctity, and that more persons are anxious to hear some new or read some beauteous thing than to read or hear about God and the great salvation. He knew that few would ever ask, "What must I do to be saved?" till they came in contact with the Bible itself; and therefore he made the Bible not only an instructive book, but an attractive one; not only true, but enticing. He filled it with marvellous incident and engaging history, with many pictures from old-world scenery, and affecting anecdotes from the patriarch times; he replenished it with stately argument and thrilling verse, and sprinkled it over with sententious wisdom and proverbial pungency; he made it a book of lofty thoughts and noble images, — a book of heavenly doctrine, but withal of earthly adaption. In preparing a guide to immortality, Infinite Wisdom gave not a dictionary nor a grammar, but a Bible,— a book, which, in trying to catch the heart of man, should captivate his taste, and which, in transforming his affections, should also expand his intellect. The pearl is of great price; but even the casket is of exquisite beauty. The sword is of ethereal temper, and nothing cuts so keen as its double edge; but there are jewels on the hilt, and fine tracery on the scabbard. The shekels are of the purest ore; but even the scrip which contains them is of a texture more curious than that the artists of earth could fashion it. The apples are gold; but even the basket is silver.

## XXX.

By THOMAS CARLYLE.—Born 1795.

*The Book of Job.*

I CALL that, apart from all theories about it, one of the grandest things ever written with pen. One feels, indeed, as if it were not Hebrew, such a noble universality, different from noble patriotism or sectarianisn, reigns in it. A noble book! all men's book! It is our first, oldest statement of the never-ending problem,—man's destiny, and God's ways with him here on earth; and all in such free, flowing outlines, grand in its sincerity, in its simplicity, in its epic melody, and repose of reconcilement. There is the seeing eye, the mildly understanding heart, so *true* every way; true eyesight and vision for all things, material things no less than spiritual; the horse,—"hast *thou* clothed his neck with thunder?" — "he *laughs* at the shaking of a spear!" Such living likenesses were never since drawn. Sublime sorrow, sublime reconciliation; oldest choral melody, as of the heart of mankind; so soft and great, as the summer midnight, as the world, with its seas and stars! There is nothing written, I think, in the Bible or out of it, of equal literary merit.

## XXXI.

### By St. Ambrose. — 340–397.

*The Varied Richness of the Bible.*

THE Bible is a sea, having its deep senses, the fulness of prophetic mystery into which many rivers have run. But there are, besides this, sweet and clear rivers, fresh springs, that yield water unto eternal life; good words, a honeycomb, acceptable sentences, which may refresh the mind of the hearers with spiritual drink, and delight them with the sweetness of moral precepts. Various, therefore, are the streams of the Bible. Thou hast what thou mayest drink first, what thou mayest drink second, and what thou mayest drink last.

## XXXII.

By Sir Walter Scott. — 1771–1832.

*The same.*

THE most learned, acute, and diligent student cannot, in the longest life, obtain an entire knowledge of this one volume. The more deeply he works the mine, the richer and more abundant he finds the ore. New light continually beams from this source of heavenly knowledge to direct the conduct and illustrate the works of God and the ways of men; and he will, at least, leave the world confessing, that the more he studied the Scriptures the fuller convictions he had of his own ignorance and of their inestimable value.

"Father of mercies, in Thy word
  What endless glory shines!
Forever be Thy name adored
  For these celestial lines.
Oh, may these heavenly pages be
  My ever dear delight!
And still new beauties may I see,
  And still increasing light!"

Mrs. Anne Steele, 1717–1778.

## XXXIII.

By Rev. George Gilfillan.

*The surpassing Richness, Unity, and Originality of the Bible.*

THE Bible is a mass of beautiful figures. Its words and its thoughts are alike poetical. It has gathered around its central truths all natural beauty and interest. It is a temple, with one altar and one God, but illuminated by a thousand varied lights, and studded with a thousand ornaments. It has substantially but one declaration to make; but it utters it in the voices of the creation. Shining forth from the excellent glory, its light has been reflected on a myriad intervening objects, till it has been at length attempered for our earthly vision. It now beams upon us at once from the heart of man and from the countenance of nature. It has arrayed itself in the charms of fiction; it has gathered new beauty from the works of creation, and new warmth and power from the very passions of clay; it has pressed into its service the animals of the forest, the flowers of the field, the stars of heaven,—all the elements of Nature. . . . Thus the quick spirit of the Book has ransacked creation to lay its treasures on Jehovah's altar; united the innumerable rays of a far-streaming glory on the little hill Calvary; and woven a garland for the bleeding brow of Immanuel, the flowers of which have been culled from the gardens of the universe.

In relation to other books, the Bible occupies a peculiar and solitary position. It is *independent* of all others; it imitates no other book; it copies none; it hardly alludes to any other, whether in praise or blame; and this is nearly as true of its later portions, when books were common, as of its earlier, when books were scarce. It proves thus its originality and power.

## XXXIV.

### By Sir William Jones. — 1646–1694.

*The Bible the richest Treasury.*

THAT great Oriental scholar said, "I have regularly and attentively read the Holy Scriptures, and am of the opinion that this volume, independently of its divine origin, contains more true sublimity, more exquisite beauty, more pure morality, more important history, and finer strains both of poetry and eloquence, than could be collected from all other books."

## XXXV.

By O. M. Mitchell, LL.D., the Devout Astronomer and Patriotic General.
1810–1862.

*The Wonderful Book.*

THE most wonderful volume in existence is, beyond a doubt, the Bible. It is wonderful for its high pretensions, for its almost incredible claims to divine origin, for its exceeding antiquity. It is wonderful in its revelation of the being of God, and in its declarations concerning the attributes of this Almighty Spirit. It is wonderful for its professed revelation of the creation of the universe, the formation of man, the origin of evil, man's fall from innocence, and his restoration to happiness. It is wonderful for its daring chronology, its positive history, its prophetic declarations. It is wonderful on account of its sublime philosophy, its exquisite poetry, its magnificent figures, its overwhelming language of description. It is wonderful for the diversity of its writers, — diverse in their attainments, countries, languages, and education. It is wonderful for its boldness, in the use of illustrations, metaphors, figures, drawn from every department of human knowledge, from natural history, from meteorology, from optics, from astronomy. It is wonderful for the superior conceptions of its writers of the grandeur and magnificence of the physical universe. It is wonderful that it has exposed itself to attack and destruction at every point of time, by every discovery of man, by the revelations of geology, chronology, history, ancient remains disembowelled from the earth, by astronomy, by the discoveries of natural history, and, above all, by the non-fulfilment of its historical predictions. And it is most of all wonderful, that up to the present time, in the opinion of hundreds of thousands of the judicious, reflecting, and reasoning among earth's inhabitants, during three thousand years since its first book was written, it has maintained its high authority, and has retained, in all this vast lapse of time, a powerful sway over the human mind.

. . . . . .

No, my friends: the analogies of Nature, applied to the moral government of God, would crush all hope in the sinful soul. There, for millions of ages, these stern laws have reigned supreme. There is no deviation, no modification, no yielding to the refractory or disobedient. All is harmony, because all is obedience. Close forever, if you will, this strange book claiming to be God's revelation; blot out for ever its lessons of creative power, God's superabounding providence, God's fatherhood and loving guardianship to man, His erring offspring, and then unseal the leaves of that mighty volume which the finger of God has written in the stars of heaven, and in these flashing letters of living light we read only the dread sentence, "The soul that sinneth, it shall surely die."

## XXXVI.

By Robert Pollok. — 1798–1827.

MOST wondrous Book! bright candle of the Lord,
Star of eternity! the only star
By which the bark of man can navigate
The sea of life, and gain the coast of bliss
Securely; only star which rose on Time,
And on its dark and troubled billows still,
As generation, drifting swiftly by,
Succeeded generation, threw a ray
Of heaven's own light, and to the hills of God —
The everlasting hills — pointed the sinner's eye.

## XXXVII.

By John Milton, the Statesman and Poet. — 1608–1674.

*The Intelligibleness and Excellence of the Bible, — of its Poetry, its Oratory, and its Politics.*

GOD has ordained His gospel to be the revelation of His power and wisdom in Christ Jesus. And this is one depth of His wisdom, that he could so plainly reveal so great a measure of it to the gross, distorted apprehension of decayed mankind. Let others, therefore, dread and shun the Scriptures for their darkness: I shall wish I may deserve to be reckoned among those who admire and dwell upon them for their clearness.

There are no songs comparable to the songs of Zion, no orations equal to those of prophets, and no politics like those which the Scriptures teach.

Better teaching
The solid rules of civil government
In their majestic, unaffected style,
Than all the oratory of Greece and Rome.
In them is plainest taught, and easiest learnt,
What makes a nation happy, and keeps it so;
What ruins kingdoms, and lays cities flat:
These only, with our law, best form a king.

## XXXVIII.

By Rev. HENRY W. BEECHER.

*The Bible, how deprived of Life and Power.*

WHAT a pin is when the diamond has dropped from its setting, that is the Bible when its emotive truths have been taken away. What a babe's clothes are when the babe has slipped out of them into death, and the mother's arms clasp only raiment, would be the Bible, if the Babe of Bethlehem, and the truths of deep-heartedness that clothed His life, should slip out of it.

## XXXIX.

By Sir CHRISTOPHER HATTON. — Died 1791.

*To know the Scriptures a Chief Duty and Interest.*

IT is justly accounted a piece of excellent knowledge to understand the law of the land and the customs of our country; but how much more excellent is it to know the statutes of heaven, and the laws of eternity, the immutable and perpetual laws of justice and righteousness! to know the will and pleasure of the great Monarch and universal King of the world! "I have seen an end of all perfection; but Thy commandments, O God! are exceedingly broad."

## XL.

By CLAUDIUS SALMASIUS. — 1596–1653.

*The Same.*

I HAVE lost an immense portion of time, — time, that most precious thing in the world! Had I but one year more, it should be spent in studying David's psalms and Paul's epistles.

## XLI.

### By Sir WALTER SCOTT.

*The only Book.*

WHILE lying at the point of death, Sir Walter said to Mr. Lockhart, his son-in-law, "Read to me." Mr. L. said, "What book shall I read?" — "What book!" replied Sir Walter: "there is but one book, — the Bible!"

## XLII.

### By VICTORIA, Queen of Great Britain.

*The Bible the Chief Means of National Prosperity.*

A FEW years ago an African prince sent an embassy with costly presents to Victoria, who, wondering at the prosperity of the country, requested to be informed as to the secret of England's greatness and glory. Having procured a very costly copy of the Bible, she bade the ambassadors bear it home to their master, with this message from her lips: "Tell the prince that this is the secret of England's greatness."

## XLIII.

By Hon. Chevalier C. K. J. Bunsen of Prussia. Born 1791.

*The Bible the only Basis of Civil and Religious Liberty.*

I HOPE that our children and our children's children will see religious liberty, not only in this land (England), and in my own country, but over the world: when the Bible and the faith of the gospel will form the basis, as it is the only basis, of civil and religious liberty; for the Bible is the only real cement of nations, and the only cement that can bind religious hearts together.

## XLIV.

By Hon. Edward Everett.—Born 1794.

*The Bible and Public Men.*

GROTIUS, the great founder of our modern science of international law, was a most assiduous student of the Bible. He was profoundly a religious man. The foundations of his moral treatise on "The Law of Nations" are laid in the Scriptures of the Old and New Testament; and the original conception of the work was in the genuine spirit of Christian philanthropy. His golden treatise on the truth of the Christian religion was intended by him as a manual for his adventurous fellow-citizens, then just engaging in the trade with the East, by aid of which they might scatter the seeds of sacred truth on distant and heathen shores.

I scarce know of a more beautiful illustration of the adaption of the religion of the Bible to the purposes of active life than is thus afforded in this model Christian statesman, who, on the one hand, continually fortifies the maxims of the public law by Scripture authority, and, on the other hand, composed a treatise on the evidences of Christianity, to be used by his seafaring countrymen in their voyages to remote regions. That was testimony to the value of the Bible.

## XLV.

### By George Washington.—1732–1799.

*The Bible supremely Beneficent.*

THE free cultivation of letters, the unbounded extension of commerce, the progressive refinement of manners, the growing liberality of sentiment, and, *above all*, the pure and benign light of *Revelation*, have had a meliorating influence on mankind, and increased the blessings of society.

Of all the dispositions and habits which lead to political prosperity, *religion* and *morality* are indispensable supports. In vain would that man claim the tribute of patriotism who should labor to subvert these pillars of human happiness, these firmest props of the duties of men and citizens. The mere politician, equally with the pious man, ought to respect them. And let us with caution indulge the supposition, that morality can be sustained without religion. Whatever may be conceded to the influence of refined education on minds of a peculiar structure, reason and experience both forbid us to expect that national morality can prevail in exclusion of religious principle.

## XLVI.

### By John Locke.—1632–1704.

*The largest Good of Mankind most fully assured by the Bible.*

THAT the Holy Scriptures are one of the greatest blessings which God bestows upon the sons of men is generally acknowledged by all who know any thing of the value and worth of them. What direction can man expect, by which he may be fortified against all enemies of his good, either within or without him, that is not there given? What encouragements would he have, which are not therein displayed before him? And what cavils can be brought against any part of truth contained therein, to which they themselves yield not a full resolve,—one place of Scripture so exactly clearing, expounding, and illustrating another? Yet, to amazement, it is observed that man, who is so highly and principally concerned in it, doth too little value it: he can weary himself in any secular affair, but diligently to search the Scriptures according to our Lord's advice, is to him tedious and burdensome.

## XLVII.

By Hon. JOSEPH C. HORNBLOWER, late Chief Justice of New Jersey. — 1777–1864.

*The same.*

LET this precious volume have its proper influence on the hearts of men, and our liberties are safe, our country blessed, and the world happy. There is not a tie that unites us to our families, not a virtue that endears us to our country, nor a hope that thrills our bosoms in the prospect of future happiness, that has not its foundation in this Bible. It is the charter of charters, the palladium of liberty, the standard of righteousness.

## XLVIII.

By Hon. WILLIAM H. SEWARD.

*The Bible essential to the true Advancement of Mankind.*

I DO not believe human society, including not merely a few persons in any state, but whole masses of men, ever has attained, or ever can attain, a high state of intelligence, virtue, security, liberty, or happiness, without the Holy Scriptures; even as the whole hope of human progress is suspended on the ever-growing influence of the Bible.

## XLIX.

By Hon. SIMON GREENLEAF, late Professor in Harvard University. — 1783–1853.

*The Sanctions of the Bible the true Source of Public and Private Security.*

OF the divine character of the Bible, I think no man, who *deals honestly with his own mind and heart,* can entertain a reasonable doubt. For myself, I must say, that, having for many years made the evidences of Christianity the subject of close and patient study, the result has been a firm and increasing conviction of the authenticity and plenary inspiration of the Bible. It is indeed the Word of God. It opens up to our view the only true source of moral obligation, or of public and private duty, and enforces these with the only sanctions that can affect the mind and reach the conscience of man; namely, the omniscience and goodness and mercy of God, and the certain retributions of the life to come. Without these sanctions, the laws are no longer observed, oaths lose their hold on the conscience, promises are violated, frauds are multiplied and moral obligation is dissolved. And these securities natural religion does not furnish: they are found in the Bible alone. In sublimity of thought, in grandeur of conception, in purity and elevation of moral principle, in the practical wisdom of its teachings, and the universality and perpetuity of their application, and, above all, in the high and important character of its themes, the Holy Bible is not even approached by any human composition. It is only this that can make men wise unto salvation.

## L.

By Hon. John McLean, late Judge of the Supreme Court of the United States.—Born 1785.

*Social Purity, Order, and Refinement secured by the Bible.*

THE laws which belong to the social relation are found in the Bible. The duties of husband and wife, parent and child, and all other connections which necessarily belong to a refined civilization, are prescribed in the Scriptures. We are commanded to love our neighbor, and in all things to do unto others as we should wish them to do unto us. If these rules were faithfully observed by individuals and communities, the highest degree of earthly happiness would be attained.

## LI.

### By Hon. Lewis Cass. — Born 1782.

*The Bible, diligently and devotedly read, a Nation's Security.*

THE youth of America have a glorious theatre of exertion before them. That they may appreciate its duties and its rewards, and may be prepared for its offers and demands, by the lessons of the sabbath and the Bible, must be the sincere wish of every one interested in the progress and prospects of our country, and especially of those who must soon pass from its councils, and see its destinies committed to a new generation. Impressed with these considerations, I earnestly hope that God's day may be hallowed, and His word studied, through this whole land, till their obligations are felt and acknowledged by all its people.

## LII.

By Hon. SAMUEL SOUTHARD. — 1787–1842.

*The Claims of the Bible on Scholars.*

OF all men, American scholars ought not to be ignorant of any thing which the Bible contains. If Cicero could declare that the laws of the Twelve Tables were worth all the libraries of the philosophers; if they were the *carmen necessarium* of the Roman youth, — how laboriously ought you to investigate its contents, and inscribe them upon your hearts! You owe to them the blessed civil institutions under which you live, and the glorious freedom which you enjoy; and, if these are to be perpetuated, it can only be by a regard to those principles. Make your scholarship subservient to the support of the same unchanging principles. Our refuge is in the firm purpose of educated and moral men. Draw, then, your rules from the only safe authority.

## LIII.

By William Tyndal, author of the version of the Bible bearing his name. — 1477 – 1536.

*Christians rendered intelligent and steadfast only by the Bible.*

WHILE I am sowing in one place, they ravage the field I have just left. I cannnot be everywhere. If Christians had the Scriptures in their own tongue, they could themselves withstand these sophists: without the Bible it is impossible to establish the laity in the truth. If God give me life, ere many years the ploughboys shall know more of the Scriptures than you do.

## LIV.

By William Chillingworth, D.D. — 1602–1644.

*The Bible the best Guide to Salvation.*

WHEN you say that unlearned and ignorant men cannot understand Scripture, I would desire you to come out of the clouds, and tell us what you mean:

whether that they cannot understand *all* Scripture; or that they cannot understand *any* Scripture; or that they cannot understand so much as is sufficient for their direction to heaven. If the first, I believe the learned are in the same case. If the second, every man's experience will confute you; for who is there that is not capable of a sufficient understanding of the story, the precepts, the promises, and the threats of the gospel? If the third, that they may understand something, but not enough for their salvation, I ask you why, then, doth St. Paul say to Timothy, "The Scriptures are able to make him wise unto salvation"?

I will love no man the less for differing in opinion from me. I am fully assured that God does not, and therefore that man ought not to, require any more of any man than this, — to believe the Scripture to be God's word, to endeavor to find the true sense of it, and to live according to it.

## LV.

By Hon. GEORGE P. MARSH.

*The Value of the one authorized English Version of the Bible.*

TO revise under present circumstances is to sectarianize, to divide the one catholic English Bible, the common standard of authority in Protestant England and America, into a dozen different revelations, each authoritative for its own narrow circle, — a counterfeit: it is a practical surrender of that human excellence of form in the English Bible, which, next to the unspeakable value of its substance, is the greatest gift which God has bestowed on the British and American people.

## LVI.

By Hon. BENJAMIN F. BUTLER, formerly Attorney-General of the United States.

*The Ideal of Human Perfection realized in the Bible.*

NOT only does the Bible inculcate, with sanctions of highest import, a system of the purest morality, but, in the person and character of our blessed Saviour, it exhibits a tangible illustration of that system. In Him we have set before us — what, till the publication of the gospel, the world had never seen — a model of feeling and action, adapted to all times, places, and circumstances; and combining so much of wisdom, benevolence, and holiness, that none can fathom its sublimity, and yet presented in a form so simple, that even a child may be made to understand, and taught to love it.

## LVII.

By Axel Oxenstierna, Chancellor of Sweden, to Whitelock, the English Ambassador. — 1583–1654.

*The Bible as a Source of Knowledge and Enjoyment.*

YOU are now in the prime of your age and vigor, and in great favor and business; but all this will leave you, and you will one day better understand and relish what I say. You will then find that there is more wisdom, truth, comfort, and pleasure in retiring, and in turning your heart from the world to the good Spirit of God, and in reading the Bible, than in all the courts and favors of princes.

## LVIII.

By Hon. DANIEL WEBSTER. — 1782–1852.

*His Two-fold Estimate of the Sacred Volume.*

TO a young friend admiring the poetry of the Bible, he said, "Ah, my friend! the poetry of Isaiah, Job, and Habakkuk is beautiful indeed; but when you have lived, as I have, sixty-nine years, you will give more for the fourteenth and seventeenth chapters of John's Gospel, or for one of the epistles, than for all the poetry of the Bible!

I have read it through many times: I now make a practice of going through it once a year. It is the book of all others for lawyers as well as divines; and I pity the man who cannot find in it a rich supply of thought, and rules for conduct.

## LIX.

By Rev. JOHN NEWTON. — 1725–1807.

*Relative Value of the Bible.*

I HAVE many books that I cannot sit down to read: they are indeed good and sound; but, like half-pence, there goes a great quantity to a small amount. There are silver books, and a very few golden books; but I have one book worth them all, called the Bible.

"This holy book I'd rather own,
Than all the gold and gems
That e'er in monarch's coffers shone,
Than all their diadems.

Nay, were the seas one chrysolite,
The earth one golden ball,
And diamonds all the stars of night,
This book was worth them all.

Ah, no! the soul ne'er found relief
In glittering hoards of wealth;
Gems dazzle not the eye of grief;
Gold cannot purchase health.

But here a blessed balm appears
To heal the deepest woe;
And those who read this book in tears,
Their tears shall cease to flow."

ANON.

## HOMAGE OF SCEPTICS TO THE BIBLE.

OF the authors of the foregoing passages, three at least — Robert Boyle, John Newton, and Richard Cecil — in early life denied the divine inspiration of the Bible. In ripened manhood, however, they were bold advocates of the gospel, and richly enjoyed its consolations. But the writers of the four selections which follow, though they may have failed of like felicity, had the rare magnanimity to acknowledge, themselves being judges, that "their rock is not as our Rock."

## LX.

By Rev. THEODORE PARKER. — 1810–1860.

*The Bible a Cherished Book.*

VIEW it in what light we may, the Bible is a very surprising phenomenon. It is read of a sabbath in all the ten thousand pulpits of our land. In all the temples of Christendom is its voice lifted up, week by week. The sun never sets on its gleaming page. It goes equally to the cottage of the plain man, and the palace of the king. It is woven into the literature of the scholar, and colors the talk of the street. The bark of the merchant cannot sail the sea without it, nor ship of war go to the conflict but the Bible is there. It blesses us when we are born; gives names to half Christendom, rejoices with us; has sympathy for our mourning; tempers our grief to finer issues. It is the better part of our sermons. It lifts man above himself: our best of uttered prayers are in its storied speech, wherewith our fathers and the patriarchs prayed. The timid man, about waking from this dream of life, looks through the glass of Scripture, and his eyes grow bright: he does not fear to stand alone, to tread the way unknown and distant, to take the death-angel by the hand, and bid farewell to wife and babes and home. Men rest on this their dearest hopes. It tells them of God and of his blessed Son, of earthly duties and of heavenly rest.

## LXI.

### By Denis Diderot.—1713–1784.

*Words of that Atheistic French Philosopher, addressed in Conversation to his Boon Companions.*

FOR a wonder, gentlemen, for a wonder, I know nobody, either in France or anywhere else, who could write and speak with more art and talent. Notwithstanding all the bad which we have said, and no doubt with good reason, of this devil of a book, I defy you all, as many as are here, to prepare a tale so simple and so touching as the tale of the passion and death of Jesus Christ; which produces the same effect, which makes a sensation as strong and as generally felt, and whose influence will be the same after so many centuries."

This unexpected speech astonished all the hearers, and was followed by a pretty long silence.

## LXII.

### By Hon. THOMAS JEFFERSON. — 1743–1826.

*The Bible improves all Earnest Readers.*

I HAVE always said, and always will say, that the studious perusal of the Sacred Volume, will make better citizens, better fathers, and better husbands.

## LXIII.

By that Sceptical and Philosophical Moralist, JEAN-JACQUES ROUSSEAU. Born 1712; died 1778.

*The Majesty and Supremacy of the Scriptures.*

I WILL confess to you that the majesty of the Scriptures strikes me with admiration, as the purity of the gospel hath its influence on my heart. Peruse the works of our philosophers, with all their pomp of diction, — how mean, how contemptible, are they, compared with the Scripture! Is it possible that a book, at once so simple and sublime, should be merely the work of man? Is it possible that the sacred personage whose history it contains should be Himself a mere man? Do we find that He assumes the tone of an enthusiast or ambitious sectary? What sweetness, what purity, in His manner! What an affecting gracefulness in His delivery! What sublimity in His maxims! What profound wisdom in His discourses! What presence of mind, what subtlety, what truth, in His replies! How great the command over His passions! Where is the man, where the philosopher, who could so live, and so die, without weakness, without ostentation? When Plato described his imaginary good man, loaded with all the shame of guilt, yet meriting the highest rewards of virtue, he described exactly the character of Jesus Christ: the resemblance was so striking, that all the fathers perceived it.

The death of Socrates, peacefully philosophizing with his friends, appears the most agreeable that could be wished for: that of Jesus, expiring in the midst of agonizing pains, abused, insulted, and accused by a whole nation, is the most horrible that could be feared. Socrates, in receiving the cup of poison, blessed, indeed, the necessary executioner who administered it; but Jesus, in the midst of excruciating tortures, prayed for His merciless tormentors. Yes: if the life and death of Socrates, which nobody presumes to doubt, were those of a sage, the life and death of Jesus were those of a God.

Shall we suppose the evangelic history a mere fiction? Indeed, my friend, it bears not the marks of fiction: on the contrary, the history of Socrates, which nobody presumes to doubt, is not so well attested as that of Jesus Christ Such a supposition, in fact, only shifts the difficulty without obviating it. It is more inconceivable that a number of persons should agree to write such a history, than that one only should furnish the subject of it. The Jewish authors were incapable of the diction, and strangers to the morality, contained in the gospel, the marks of whose truth are so striking and inimitable, that the inventor would be a more astonishing character than the hero.

# PART SECOND.

---

# HOMAGE

OF

# EMINENT PERSONS

TO

# THE BOOK,

IN

*WORDS APOLOGETIC AND EVIDENTIAL.*

---

"*'Tis Revelation satisfies all doubts,*
*Explains all mysteries, except her own.*"

*"All Scripture is given by Inspiration of God."*

# PART II.

## WORDS APOLOGETIC AND EVIDENTIAL.

IS the Bible credible? is it divinely inspired? can its credibility and inspiration be firmly established? are questions which every reader of it is bound to settle for himself; and there are three ways of doing this, neither of which conflicts with the others. There are advantages, moreover, belonging to each.

The first is the *literary* way, which few besides scholars find time and disposition to travel. Yet every divergent road, and byway as well, will yield its wealth of confirmatory proof to reward diligent and wakeful explorers.

The second mode of becoming assured of the divine origin of the Bible is by *experience* Profound philosophers and unlettered peasants may be equals here. Historic testimony and erudite reasoning are here out of the account. Men know that the Bible claims to be from God, and that to obey its moral teachings is right, fitting, and beautiful. The Saviour, moreover, declared His doctrines to be from God; and He gave mankind this one infallible rule for testing their divinity: "If *any* man will *do His will* [the will of the Father which He taught] he shall *know* of the doctrine, whether it be of God, or whether I speak of myself."

Another and third process of arriving at a firm conviction that the Bible is a record of inspired and infallible truth, *is by thoughtfully weighing the arguments, suggestions, and opinions of persons eminent for wisdom and worth.* This is no blind submission to authority. It is, rather, the acceptance of manifold challenges to manly and earnest reflection. While one thus responsibly decides as to the value of the maxims, hints, and opinions of another, he may also employ them to elaborate theories and conclusions peculiarly his own: even as the great naturalist Cuvier reached his splendid results in comparative anatomy, by reconstructing animals of a former era from no other data than here and there a fossil tooth or bone.

I.

From Barker's Bible. — 1594.

HERE is the spring where waters flowe,
  To quench our heate of sinne;
Here is the tree where trueth doth grow,
  To lead our lives therein;
Here is the judge that stints the strife,
  Where men's devices faille;
The tidings of salvation deare
  Come to our eares from hence;
The fortress of our faith is here,
  And shield of our defence.

II.

By Monsieur F. P. G. Guizot, the Philosophic Statesman and Historian. — Born 1787.

*The Bible the best Bulwark of the Faith.*

THE Christian faith has been, and is still, very fiercely and obstinately attacked. How many efforts have been and are still made; how many books, serious or frivolous, able or silly, have been and are spread incessantly,—in order to destroy it in men's minds! Where has this redoubtable struggle been supported with the greatest energy and success? and where has Christian faith been best defended? There, where the reading of the Sacred Books is a general and assiduous part of the public worship; there, where it takes place in the interior of families, and in solitary meditation. It is the Bible, the Bible itself, which combats and triumphs most efficaciously in the war between incredulity and belief.

## III.

By Sir Isaac Newton, the Astronomer and Philosopher.—1642–1727.

*The Bible the most Sublime and Credible of Books.*

WE account the Scriptures of God to be the most sublime philosophy.

I find more sure marks of authenticity in the Bible than in any profane history whatever.

## IV.

By Rev. HENRY ROGERS, the Essayist.—Born 1814.

*That the Gospels are Fictions, Incredible.*

AS Lord Bacon said that he would sooner believe "all the fables of the Talmud, than that this universal frame was without a mind," so I could sooner believe all those fables, than that minds that could *only* produce Talmuds should have conceived such *fictions* as the gospel. I would as soon believe that some dull chronicler of the Middle Ages composed Shakspeare's plays, or a ploughman had written "Paradise Lost;" only that, to parallel the present case, we ought to believe that four ploughmen wrote four "Paradise Losts!" Nay, I would as soon believe that most laughable theory of learned folly, that the monks of the Middle Ages compiled all the classics!

The New Testament is not more different from the writings of Jews, or superior to them, than it is different from the writings of the Fathers, and superior to them. It stands alone, like the Peak of Teneriffe. The Alps amidst the flats of Holland would not present a greater contrast than the New Testament and the Fathers. And, the further we come down, the less capable morally, and nearly as incapable intellectually, do the rapidly degenerating Christians appear of producing such a *fiction* as the New Testament; so that, if it be asked whether it was not possible that some Christians of after-times might have *forged* these books, one must say, with Paley, that they *could* not.

## V.

### By Rev. William Ellery Channing, D.D. 1780–1842.

*The Divine Reality of the Gospels.*

THE Gospels must be true: they were drawn from a living original; they were founded on reality. The character of Jesus is not a fiction. He was what He claimed to be, and what His followers attested. Nor is this all. Jesus not only was, He is still, the Son of God, the Saviour of the world.

## VI.

### By Joseph Angus, D.D.

*The Character of Christ proves the Scriptures to be Divine.*

THE Bible is the one book which claims "God for its author, unmixed truth for its contents, and salvation for its end." If we admit the authority of our Lord as a divine Teacher, the authority of the Bible is established. If we deny the authority of the Bible, we deny the truth of some of His most frequent teachings, and with it the divinity of His mission.

. . . . . . . . .

Among the most decisive proofs of the divine origin of the Scriptures is the character of Christ. It is a proof, however, rather to be felt than to be described; and its force will be in proportion to the tone of moral sentiment in the reader. Holy and pure minds will feel it more than others; and such as are like Nathaniel, the "Israelite, indeed, in whom is no guile," will exclaim with him, "Rabbi, Thou art the Son of God; Thou art the King of Israel."

## VII.

### By Prof. Calvin E. Stowe, D.D.

*Cavillers against Divine Inspiration.*

THESE men say, that the Bible is no more inspired than the writings of Homer and Shakspeare, and other great men whom God has fitted to be the instructors of mankind. Well, then, let us try and see. Let us, for a while, use Homer and Shakspeare, instead of the Bible, — say night and morning, in our family prayers; when we meet in the house of God for His worship; in the hours of sickness and calamity and distress; at funerals, when all our earthly hopes are blighted, and we lay our dearest friends in the grave: let us then, instead of reading the Bible, take a few passages from Homer and Shakspeare. How long do you think this would last, before we should be glad to get back to our Bible again?

"God's book, rash doubter, holds the plain record:
Dar'st talk of hopes and doubts against that Word?
Dar'st palter with it in a quibbling sense?
That book shall judge thee when thou passest hence.
Then, — with thy spirit from the body freed, —
Then shalt thou know, see, feel, what's life indeed!"

R. H. Dana.

## VIII.

### By D. Simpson.

*The Bible Divinely Inspired.*

THE Bible must be the invention either of *good men or angels, bad men or devils, or of God.*

It could not be the invention of *good men or angels;* for they neither would nor could make a book, and tell lies all the time they were writing, saying, *Thus saith the Lord,* when it was their own invention.

It could not be the invention of *bad men or devils*; for they could not make a book which commands all duty, forbids all sin, and condemns their souls to all eternity. We therefore draw this conclusion: *The Bible must have been given by Divine Inspiration.*

## IX.

### By S. T. Coleridge. — 1772–1834.

*Proof from Self-consciousness.*

I KNOW the Bible is inspired, because it finds me at greater depths of my being than any other book.

## X.

### By Rev. R. Chevenix Trench. — 1807.

*Unity of the Bible.*

NO single age beheld the birth of this book, which was well nigh two thousand years ere it was fully formed and had reached its full completion. Nor can its unity, if it exist, be accounted for from its having had but one class of men for its human authors; since men not of one class alone, but of many, and those the widest apart, — kings and herdsmen, wise men and simple, have alike brought their one stone or more, and been permitted to build them into this august dome and temple which God, through so many ages, was rearing to its glorious height.

## XI.

### By Rev. Albert Barnes. — Born 1798.

*The Wonderful Unity of the Bible.*

YOU can not *bind up* the literature of any other people, making one organic volume, as the Bible is bound up. You cannot thus bind up Grecian literature in one volume. You have Homer, *and* Hesiod, *and* Herodotus, *and* Thucydides, *and* Aristotle, *and* Plato, *and* Sophocles, *and* Æschylus; but they would not, and could not, make one volume, having a beginning, a middle, and an end. There is no reason why it should *begin* thus, why it should *advance* thus; and there is no catastrophe at its close. It is *one* book. They are *many* books. There *is* no unity. They are not the production of one *class* of men, except as the Greeks in general were distinguished from the rest of mankind.

## XII.

### By Francis (Lord Verulam) Bacon.—1561–1626.

*The Bible the best Revealer of God, and the best Source of Theology.*

THY creatures have been my books, but Thy Scriptures much more: I have sought Thee in the courts, fields, and gardens, but I have found Thee in Thy temples.

. . . . . . . .

I am persuaded, that if the choicest and best of those observations upon texts of Scripture which have been made dispersedly in sermons within the island of Britain, by the space of these forty years and more, had been set down in a continuance, it had been the best work on divinity which had been written since the apostles' times.

## XIII.

### By J. W. V. Goethe. — 1749–1832.

*The Bible and Reason.*

THE farther the ages advance in cultivation, the more can the Bible be used, partly as the foundation, partly as the means, of education, not, of course, by superficial, but by really wise men.

## XIV.

### By Johann Kepler. — 1571–1630.

*The Language of the Scriptures Popular, not Scientific.*

WE astronomers say, with the common people, the planets stand still or go down; the sun rises and sets. How much less should we require that the Scriptures of divine inspiration, setting aside the common modes of speech, should shape their words according to the model of the natural sciences, and, by employing a dark and inappropriate phraseology about things which surpass the comprehension of those whom it designs to instruct, perplex the simple people of God, and thus obstruct its own way towards the attainment of the far more exalted object at which it aims!

## XV.

### By M. F. Maury, LL.D. — Born 1806.

*The Bible and Science.*

I HAVE been blamed by men of science, both in this country and in England, for quoting the Bible in confirmation of the doctrines of physical geography. The Bible, they say, was not written for scientific purposes, and is therefore of no authority. I beg pardon: the Bible *is* authority for every thing it touches. What would you think of the historian who should refuse to consult the historical records of the Bible, because the Bible was not written for the purpose of history? The Bible is true, and science is true; and when your man of science, with vain and hasty conceit, announces the discovery of a disagreement between them, rely upon it, the fault is not with the witness or his records, but with the "worm" who essays to interpret evidence which he does not understand.

When I, a pioneer in one department of this beautiful science, discover the truths of revelation and the truths of science reflecting light one upon the other, and each sustaining the other, how can I, as a truth-loving, knowledge-seeking man, fail to point out the beauty, and rejoice in the discovery? And were I to suppress the emotions with which such discoveries ought to stir the soul, the waves of the sea would lift up their voice, and the very stones of the earth cry out against me.

## XVI.

By BENJAMIN SILLIMAN, M.D., LL.D., late Professor in Yale College. — 1779–1864.

*The Bible not contradicted by Science.*

THE relation of geology, as well as astronomy, to the Bible, *when both are well understood*, is that of perfect harmony. The Bible nowhere limits the age of our globe, while its chronology assigns a recent origin to the human race; and geology not only confirms the truth of the history of man, but it affords decisive evidence that the Genesis presents a true statement of the progress of the terrestrial arrangements, and of the introduction of living beings in the order in which their fossil remains are found entombed in the strata. The Word and the works of God cannot be in conflict; and, the more they are studied, the more perfect will their harmony appear.

## XVII.

By Archbishop RICHARD WHATELY, D.D.— Born 1789.

*That there are Difficulties in the Bible, Reasonable.*

THAT there are difficulties in many parts of Scripture, and that there is consequent danger of mischievous perversion, is undeniable, and is, indeed, what analogy would prepare us to expect; for if the Scriptures could be properly understood without any trouble, and were incapable of perversion to bad purposes, they would be extremely unlike the rest of God's gifts. But the difficulties of Scripture, as well as the danger of misinterpreting it, are evidently an additional reason for diligence in the study of it.

## XVIII.

### By JOSEPH BUTLER, Bishop of Durham.—1692–1752.

*On the Difficulties in the Scriptures.*

ORIGEN has observed, with singular sagacity, that he who believes the Scripture to have proceeded from Him who is the author of nature, may well expect to find the same sort of difficulties in it as are found in the constitution of nature; and, in a like way of reflection, it may be added, that he who denies the Scripture to have been from God upon account of these difficulties, may, for the very same reason, deny the world to have been from Him.

Christianity being supposed either true or credible, it is unspeakable irreverence, and really the most presumptuous rashness, to treat it as a light matter. It can never justly be esteemed of little consequence till it be positively supposed false. Nor do I know a higher or more important obligation which we are under *than that of examining most seriously into the evidence of it, supposing its credibility, and of embracing it upon supposition of its truth.*

## XIX.

By Prof. F. A. G. THOLUCK.—Born 1799.

*The Chief Ground of Difficulty in comprehending the Scriptures.*

THE reason why we find so many dark places in the Bible is, for the most part, because there are so many dark places in our hearts. It belongs to the nature of this Book, that it was written for all men of every time, and for all the experiences of each single human heart.

## XX.

### By Thomas Fuller, D.D. — 1608–1661.

*An Aptness to understand the Scriptures gradually acquired.*

LORD, this morning I read a chapter in the Bible, and therein observed a memorable passage, whereof I never took notice before. Why now, and no sooner, did I see it? Formerly my eyes were as open, and the letters as legible. Is there not a thin veil laid over Thy word, which is more rarefied by reading, and at last wholly worn away? Or was it because I came with more appetite than before? The milk was always there in the breast; but the child till now was not hungry enough to find out the teat. I see the oil of Thy word will never cease increasing whilst any bring an empty barrel. The Old Testament will still be a New Testament to him who comes with a fresh desire of information.

Within that awful volume lies
The mystery of mysteries.
Happiest they, of human race,
To whom our God has granted grace
To read, to fear, to hope, to pray,
To lift the latch, and force the way;
And better had they ne'er been born
Who read to doubt, or read to scorn.

Sir Walter Scott.

## XXI.

By Rev. John Owen, D.D., — 1616-1683.

*The Self-evidencing Powers of the Bible.*

THERE are two things to be considered in the doctrine of Scripture, which to me seem not only to persuade, but to convince, the understanding of unprejudiced men of its divine original. Its universal suitableness, upon its first clear discovery, to all the entanglements and perplexities of the souls of men, in reference to their relation to and dependence on God. Now, there are three things that all of mankind, not naturally brutish, are perplexed with in relation to God: how they may worship Him as they ought; how they may be reconciled and at peace with Him, or have an atonement for that guilt of which they are naturally sensible; what is the nature of true blessedness, and how they may attain to it.

Another consideration of like efficacy may be taken from a brief view of the whole Scripture, with the design of it. The consent of parts, or *harmony* of Scripture with itself, and every part of it with each other and with the whole, is commonly pleaded as an evidence of its divine original. Thus much certainly it doth evince, beyond all possible contradiction, — that the whole proceedeth from one and the same principle, hath the same author, and He wise, discerning, able to comprehend the whole compass of what He intended to deliver and reveal. Otherwise, that oneness of spirit, design, and aim, in unspeakable diversity of means of its delivery, that absolute correspondency of it to itself and unlikeness to any thing else, could not have been attained.

## XXII.

### By Hugo Grotius. — 1583–1645.

*The Books of the Old Testament Genuine.*

BUT there is no need for us Christians to doubt the credibility of these books, because there are testimonies in our books, out of almost every one of them, the same as they are found in Hebrew. Nor did Christ, when he reproved many things in the teachers of the Law, and in the Pharisees of His time, ever accuse them of falsifying the books of Moses and the Prophets, or of using supposititious or altered books.

And it can never be proved, or made credible, that after Christ's time the Scripture should be corrupted in any thing of moment, if we do but consider how far and wide the Jewish nation, which everywhere kept these books, was dispersed over the whole world.

## XXIII.

### By Joseph Addison. — 1672–1719.

*The Jews, as a People, unconsciously Witness to the Divinity of the Bible.*

THE firm *adherence* of the Jews to their religion is no less remarkable than their *numbers* and *dispersion*. If we consider what providential reason may be assigned for these three particulars, we shall find that their numbers, dispersion, and adherence to their religion, have furnished every age, and every nation of the world, with the strongest arguments for the Christian faith, not only as these very particulars are foretold of them, but as they themselves are the depositaries of these and all other prophecies which tend to their confusion.

Their number furnishes us with a sufficient cloud of witnesses, that attest the truth of the Old Bible. Their dispersion spreads these witnesses through all parts of the world. The adherence to their religion makes their testimony unquestionable. Had the whole body of Jews been converted to Christianity, we should certainly have thought all the prophecies of the Old Testament, that relate to the coming and history of our blessed Saviour, forged by Christians, and have looked upon them, with the prophecies of the *Sibyls*, as made many years after the events they pretend to foretell.

## XXIV.

By John Jewel, Bishop. — 1522–1574.

*Wonderful Preservation of the Bible.*

CITIES fall, kingdoms come to nothing, empires fade away as smoke. Where is Numa, Minos, Lycurgus? Where are their books? and what is become of their laws? But that this Book no tyrant should have been able to consume, no tradition to choke, no heretic maliciously to corrupt; that it should stand unto this day, amid the wreck of all that is human, without the alteration of one sentence so as to change the doctrine taught therein, — surely there is a very singular providence, claiming our attention in a most remarkable manner.

## XXV.

### By NAPOLEON BONAPARTE. — 1769-1821.

*Paganism contrasted with Christianity and with the Christian Scriptures.*

PAGANISM is the work of man. One can here read imbecility. What do these gods, so boastful, know more than other mortals; these legislators, Greek or Roman; this Numa, this Lycurgus; these priests of India, or of Memphis; this Confucius; this Mohammed? — absolutely nothing. They have made a perfect chaos of morals. There is not one among them all who has said any thing new in reference to our future destiny, to the soul, to the essence of God, to the creation. Enter the sanctuaries of paganism, you there find perfect chaos, a thousand contradictions, war between the gods, impurity and abomination adored, all sorts of corruption festering in the thick shades, with the rotten wood, the idol, and the priest. Does this honor God, or does it dishonor Him? Are these religions and these gods to be compared with Christianity?

Truth should embrace the universe. Such is Christianity, — the only religion which destroys sectional prejudices; the only one which proclaims the unity and the absolute brotherhood of the whole human family; the only one which is purely spiritual; in fine, the only one which assigns to all, without distinction, for a true country, the bosom of the Creator, God. Christ proved that He was the Son of the Eternal by His disregard of time. All His doctrines signify only and the same thing, — eternity.

The gospel is more than a book: it is a living being, with an action, a power, which invades every thing that opposes its extension. Behold! it is upon this table, — this book [the Bible] surpassing all others: I never omit to read it, and every day with new pleasure.

Nowhere is to be found such a series of

beautiful ideas,—admirable moral maxims, which pass before us like the battalions of a celestial army, and which produce in our soul the same emotions which one experiences in contemplating the infinite expanse of the skies, resplendent in a summer's night with all the brilliance of the stars. Not only is our mind absorbed; it is controlled: and the soul can never go astray with this book for its guide.

## XXVI.

By Rev. GARDINER SPRING, D.D.—Born 1785.

*The Religion of the Bible.*

GOD is light. So is the religion of the Bible. It has no fellowship with darkness. Not one of its graces springs from stupidity or ignorance, but all of them from the knowledge of God. False religions are founded in darkness. The religion of the Bible, like its Author, dwells in light. God also is love; and so is the religion of the Bible. "He that dwelleth in love, dwelleth in God, and God in him."

## XXVII.

By Rev. J. A. Macduff.

*The Bible the Book of Books.*

AH, *Philosophy!* thou hast never yet, as *this* book, taught a man how to die. *Reason!* with thy flickering torch, thou hast never yet guided to such sublime mysteries, such comforting truths as these. *Science!* thou hast penetrated the arcana of nature, sunk thy shafts into the earth's recesses, unburied its stores, counted its strata, measured the height of its massive pillars, down to the very pedestals of primeval granite. Thou hast tracked the lightning, traced the path of the tornado, uncurtained the distant planet, foretold the coming of the comet, and the return of the eclipse. But thou hast never been able to gauge the depth of man's soul, or to answer the question, " What must I do to be saved?"

No, no! this antiquated volume is still the "Book of books," the oracle of oracles, the beacon of beacons, the poor man's treasury, the child's companion, the sick man's health, the dying man's life; shallows for the infant to walk in, depths for giant intellect to explore and adore! Philosophy, if she would own it, is indebted here for the noblest of her maxims; Poetry for the loftiest of her themes. Painting has gathered here her noblest inspirations. Music has ransacked these golden stores for the grandest of her strains.

## XXVIII.

### By James Beattie. — 1735–1803.

*The Gospel sublimely and benignantly Pure and Rational.*

THERE is not a book on earth so favorable to all the *kind* and the *sublime* affections, or so *unfriendly* to *hatred* and *persecution*, to *tyranny*, *injustice*, and *every sort* of *malevolence*, as is the *gospel.* It breathes throughout *mercy*, *benevolence*, and *peace.*

Such of the doctrines of the gospel as are level to human capacity appear to be agreeable to the purest truth and soundest morality. All the genius and learning of the heathen world, all the penetration of Pythagoras, Socrates, and Aristotle, had never been able to produce such a system of *moral duty*, and so *rational* an account of Providence and of man, as is to be found in the New Testament.

## XXIX.

By Francis Wayland, D.D.

*The Divinity of the Scriptures evinced by their Influences.*

THAT the truths of the Bible have the power of awakening an intense moral feeling in man under every variety of character, learned or ignorant, civilized or savage; that they make bad men good, and send a pulse of healthful feeling through all the domestic, civil, and social relations; that they teach men to love right, and hate wrong, and to seek each other's welfare, as the children of one common Parent; that they control the baleful passions of the human heart, and thus make man proficient in the science of self-government; and, finally, that they teach him to aspire after a conformity to a Being of infinite holiness, and fill him with hopes infinitely more purifying, more exalted, more suited to his nature, than any other which this world has ever known, are facts as incontrovertible as the laws of philosophy, or the demonstrations of mathematics.

## XXX.

By EUSEBIUS, Bishop of Cæsarea.—264–340.

*The same.*

IF you desire any other proofs of the excellence of the truth, showing that it is not of mortal nature, but is really the Word of God, and that power of God in the Saviour has been revealed, not by words only, but by deeds, attend now. What king, philosopher, lawgiver, or prophet, ever effected so much, that he should be preached throughout the whole earth; and who bade his disciples go and testify for him, and suffer for his sake, and with the word brought the deed to pass? What prince, what armies, ever, in spite of the constant opposition of all, went and prospered every where. Who ever before had a people after his own name, not in a corner of the world, but among all, barbarians and Greeks alike; and, by the doctrines which he taught (being confirmed by deeds), turned men, yea, even the Egyptians, from idolatry?

## XXXI.

### By J. W. V. Goethe. — 1749 - 1832.

*The Scriptures a World-vanquishing Power: their Writers heroically True.*

THE mighty power of these books, and their accounts, have been tested and proved. They have overcome paganism; they have conquered Greece, Rome, and barbarous Europe; they are on the way of conquering the world. And the sincerity of the authors is no less certain than the power of the books. We may contest the learning and critical sagacity of the first historians of Jesus Christ; but it is impossible to contest their good faith: it shines from their words; they believed what they said; they sealed their assertions with their blood.

"Whence, but from heaven, could men unskilled in arts,
In several ages born, in several parts,
Weave such agreeing truths? or how, or why,
Should all conspire to cheat us with a lie?
Unasked their pains, ungrateful their advice,
Starving their gain, and martyrdom their price."

Dryden.

PART THIRD.

---

# HOMAGE

OF

# EMINENT PERSONS

TO

# THE BOOK

*AS A SCHOOL-BOOK.*

---

"THE CHILD IS FATHER OF THE MAN."

*"From a child thou hast known the Holy Scriptures, which are able to make thee wise unto salvation through faith in Christ Jesus."*

# PART III.

## HOMAGE TO THE BOOK AS A SCHOOL-BOOK

*"The Child is Father of the Man."*

### A REASON RENDERED.

AS this little volume is designed especially for those who must soon wield the destinies of the Republic, it has been deemed proper to unite the following testimonies, showing the value of the Bible as a school-book, with the foregoing compilations.

Our nation has just entered on a new era of its history. Its past prosperity is clearly traceable to the reverence of its founders, and of our fathers, for the Holy Scriptures. Had there been a *growth* of veneration for the principles which they teach, and for the sacredness of a civil oath, equal to that of our population, our soil would not of late have been saturated with the blood of so many thousands of brave brothers and sons; and, if the future of the Republic is to be truly honorable and happy, the children and youth, while in a course of training, must become reverently familiar with the teachings of the Bible! *What influence it shall have in our popular education our young men must decide.* This is a matter challenging earnest and sober thought. The profound convictions and the mature decisions of men whose uprightness, sagacity, and experience eminently fitted them to judge, are here recorded. To evade this question is to be reckless of the public weal. To neglect the Bible is disloyalty to God, to the welfare of mankind and of our National Government, whose preservation has cost untold sufferings, and rivers of blood.

It is not claimed that *theology* shall be taught in our public schools. Theology is man-made, but the Bible is God-given. Though suns and stars shone for ages before there was a true astronomy, before men found out the laws and periods of their motions, who ever denied or doubted the beauty and benefits of their light? As the genial beams of the sun quicken and cherish every form of vegetable and animal life, while they both beget and reveal beauty; so the Bible is the sun of the moral world, banishing the darkness of ignorance and sin from the mind and heart, and kindling a new, holy, and happy life in all who lovingly heed its teachings. Educate without the Bible! Keep from the minds of the young the great truths of immortality! Bound their vision by things perishable, deprive them of the best spurs to goodness, and let them be familiar only with the cold verities of natural science, with the forms and figures of speech, and with the grovelling range of worldly ideas! More wisely may we believe that the pale moonbeams alone can clothe our gardens with fragrant and beautiful blossoms, and our fields with a rich fruitage of ripened corn, than look for symmetry, loveliness, and force of character, to a process of training not cheered and energized by the light which shines from the Sacred Oracles.

## I.

### By Dr. Martin Luther, the Reformer.—1483–1546.

*The Bible should be Foremost.*

ABOVE all things, let the Scriptures be the chief and most frequently used reading-book, both in primary and in high schools. Is it not proper and right that every human being, by the time he has reached his tenth year, should be familiar with the Holy Gospels, in which the very core and marrow of his life is bound? But where the Scriptures do not bear sway, there I would counsel none to send his child; for every institution will degenerate where God's word is not in daily exercise.

## II.

### By John Locke, the Mental Philosopher.—1632–1704.

*The Plainest Parts of the Bible to be read First.*

WHAT an odd jumble of thoughts must a child have in his head, if he have any at all, such as he should have concerning religion, who, in his tender age, reads all the parts of the Bible indifferently, as the Word of God, without any distinction! I am apt to think that this, in some men, has been the very reason why they never had clear and distinct thoughts of it all their lifetime.

The reading of the whole Scriptures indifferently is what I think very inconvenient for children, till, after having been made acquainted with the plainest fundamental parts of it, they have got some kind of general view of what they ought principally to believe and practise, which yet, I think (they ought to receive in the very words of the Scripture), and not in such as men, prepossessed by systems and analogies, are apt in this case to make use of, and force upon them.

"Great God! with wonder and with praise
  On all thy works I look;
But still thy wisdom, power, and grace
  Shine brightest in thy Book.
Here are my choicest treasures hid;
  Here my best comfort lies;
Here my desires are satisfied,
  And hence my hopes arise."

WATTS.

## III.

By Benjamin Rush, M.D. — 1745–1813.

THAT eminent man began a treatise, urging the use of the Bible in schools, with the following assumptions: —

1. That Christianity is the only true and perfect religion; and that, in proportion as mankind adopt its principles and obey its precepts, they will be wise and happy.
2. That a better knowledge of this religion is to be acquired by reading the Bible than in any other way.
3. That the Bible contains more knowledge necessary to man in his present state than any other book.
4. That knowledge is most durable, and religious instruction most useful, when imparted in early life.
5. That the Bible, when not read in schools, is seldom read in any subsequent period of life.

My arguments in favor of the use of the Bible as a school-book are founded, *first in the constitution of the human mind.*

1. The *memory* is the first faculty which

opens in the minds of children. Of how much consequence, then, must it be to impress it with the great truths of Christianity before it is pre-occupied with less interesting subjects!

2. There is a peculiar *aptitude* in the minds of children for *religious* knowledge. I have constantly found them, in the first six or seven years of their lives, more inquisitive upon religious subjects than upon any others; and an ingenious instructor of youth has informed me, that he has found young children more capable of receiving just ideas upon the most difficult tenets of religion, than upon the most simple branches of human knowledge. It would be strange if it were otherwise; for God creates all his means to suit his ends. There must, of course, be a fitness between the human mind and the truths which are essential to its happiness.

3. We are subject, by a general law of our natures, to what is called *habit*. Now, if the study of the Scriptures be necessary to our happiness at any time of our lives, the sooner we begin to read them, the more we shall be attached to them; for it is a characteristic of

all habits to become easy, strong, and agreeable by repetition.

4. There is a wonderful property in the *memory*, which enables it, in old age, to *recover* the knowledge it had acquired in early life, after it had been apparently forgotten for forty or fifty years. Of how much consequence, then, must it be to fill the mind with that species of knowledge in childhood and youth, which, when *recalled* in the decline of life, will support the soul under the infirmities of age, and approaching death! The Bible is the only book which is capable of affording this support in old age; and it is for this reason that we find it resorted to with so much diligence and pleasure by such old people as have read it in early life.

My *second* argument in favor of the use of the Bible in schools is founded on an *implied command of God, and upon the practice of several of the wisest nations of the world.*

In the sixth chapter of Deuteronomy, we find the following words, which are directly to our purpose: "And thou shalt love the Lord thy God with all thy heart, and with all thy soul, and with all thy might. And these words, which I command thee this day, shall be in thy heart; and thou shalt teach them diligently to thy children, and shalt talk of them when thou sittest down, and when thou risest up."

It appears, moreover, from the history of the Jews, that they flourished as a nation in proportion as they honored and read the books of Moses, which contained the only revelation that God had made to the world. The law was not only neglected, but lost, during the general profligacy of manners which accompanied the long and wicked reign of Manasseh; but the discovery of it, amid the rubbish of the temple, by Josiah, and its subsequent general use, were followed by a return of national virtue and prosperity. We read further of the wonderful effects which the reading of the law by Ezra, after his return from his captivity in Babylon, had upon the Jews. They hung upon his lips with tears, and showed the sincerity of their repentance by their general reformation.

But the benefits of an early and general

acquaintance with the Bible were not confined to the Jewish nation. They have appeared in many countries in Europe since the Reformation. The industry, and habits of order, which distinguished many of the German nations are derived from their early instruction in the principles of Christianity by means of the Bible. In Scotland, and in parts of New England where the Bible has been long used as a school-book, the inhabitants are among the most enlightened in religion and science, the most strict in morals, and the most enterprising and efficient in human affairs, of any people whose history has come to my knowledge.

I wish to be excused for repeating here, that, if the Bible did not convey a single direction for the attainment of future happiness, it should be read in our schools *in preference to all other books*, from its containing the greatest portion of that kind of knowledge which is calculated to produce private and public temporal happiness.

I know there is an objection among many people to teaching children doctrines of any kind, because they are liable to be controverted; but let us not be wiser than our Maker. If moral precepts alone could have reformed mankind, the mission of the Son of God into our world would have been unnecessary. The perfect morality of the gospel rests upon a doctrine, which, though often controverted, has never been refuted: I mean the vicarious life and death of the Son of God. This sublime and ineffable doctrine delivers us from the absurd hypotheses of modern philosophers concerning the foundation of moral obligation, and fixes it upon the eternal and self-moving principle of LOVE. It concentrates a whole system of ethics in a single text of Scripture, —"A new commandment I give unto you, that ye love one another, even as I have loved you."

In contemplating the political institutions of the United States, I lament that we waste so much time and money in *punishing* crimes, and take so little pains to *prevent* them. We profess to be republicans, and yet we neglect the only means of establishing and perpetuating our republican forms of government; that is, the universal education of our youth in the principles of Christianity by means of the Bible: for this divine book, above all others, favors that equality among mankind, that respect for just laws, and all those sober and frugal virtues which constitute the soul of republicanism.

"I saw once more that aspect bright,—
The boy's meek head was bowed
In silence o'er the Book of light;
And like a golden cloud,
The still cloud of a pictured sky,
His locks drooped round it lovingly.

And if my heart had deemed him fair
When in the fountain glade,
A creature of the sky and air,
Almost on wings he played,
Oh, how much holier beauty now
Lit the young human being's brow!—

The being born to toil, to die,
To break forth from the tomb
Unto far nobler destiny
Than waits the skylark's plume.
I saw him, in the thoughtful hour,
Win the first knowledge of his dower."

Mrs. Hemans.

## IV.

### By JOSEPH STORY, LL.D. — 1779-1845.

*Restraints on Liberty of Speech and on Liberty of Reading the Bible.*

IT is notorious that even to this day, in some foreign countries, it is a crime to speak on any subject, religious, philosophical, or political, what is contrary to the received opinions of the government or the institutions of the country, however laudable may be the design, and however virtuous may be the motive. . . . The Bible itself, the common inheritance, not merely of Christendom, but of the world, has been put exclusively under the control of government, and has not been allowed to be seen or heard or read, except in a language unknown to the common inhabitants of the country. To publish a translation in the vernacular tongue has been in former times a flagrant offence.

## V.

By VICTOR COUSIN, the French Philosopher. 1792.

*From his Report concerning Public Instruction in Germany.*

THE general system of instruction is grounded on the Bible as translated by Luther, the catechism, and Scripture history: and every wise man will rejoice in this; for, with three-fourths of the population, morality can be instilled only through the medium of religion. Luther's forcible and popular translation of the Bible is in circulation from one end of Protestant Germany to the other, and has greatly aided in the moral and religious education of the people.

## VI.

By GEORGE CHRISTIAN KNAPP, D.D., Professor of Theology in the University of Halle. — 1753–1825.

*How to exterminate Christianity.*

THE most direct way to render Christianity obsolete is to take the Bible from the hands of the common people. And already have we begun to experience the evils resulting from the efforts of some modern teachers to banish the reading of the Scriptures, especially of the Old Testament, from our *schools*, or at least diminish the degree of attention formerly paid to them.

## VII.

By Sir ROBERT PEEL. — 1788–1850.

*Sectarian Prejudice must not exclude Religious Instructions from Schools.*

(*From a Speech delivered* 1827.)

THERE is a great movement of the public mind relative to public education. All parties, of whatever creed or religious denomination, are beginning to be convinced that there has been, upon the part of all of us, a great deficiency in that respect. We have permitted our religious differences to operate against education; and it has now become necessary that that great object of national education shall be obtained by a sacrifice, on the part of all of us, of some of those *scruples* which have hitherto prevented it.

## VIII.

### By Rev. George B. Cheever, D.D,

*The Bible not Sectarian.*

THE Bible is older than any sect in the world. The Bible is the only Catholicity, the only form in which religion can be taught without a sectarian religious bias; and that is a great and mighty reason why it *should* be taught, or enter in some way as an acknowledged divine element into our public-school system. Our English translation, which the learned Selden called the "best version in the world," is not a Protestant translation, nor a Protestant Bible; but it is simply the people's Bible, the word of God in English, for those who speak the English tongue. If no Bible but the original Greek and Hebrew were the word of God, then none but Greeks and Hebrews *have* the word of God. This stigmatizing of our English translation as the Protestant version is a poor trick, resorted to in order to banish the word of God from our schools. The word of God in English is no more the Protestant Bible or the Protestant version, than the science of Algebra in English is Protestant algebra, or of astronomy the Protestant astronomy; no more than the stars in America are Protestant stars, or the sun a Protestant sun. Both the works of God and the word of God are God's truth.

## IX.

### By Rev. J. H. Seelye, in the Bibliotheca Sacra.

*The Bible the Source and Security of our Institutions.*

NOW, as already indicated, the religion of this country is that of the Bible. No one can properly dispute this. No matter whether the Bible be true or false: it is the exponent of our religion, and is the book containing the principles which have moulded all our civil institutions. It is that which gives character and force and stability to our government and laws. You might as well take out the heart from the body, and suppose that it would be a living body still, as to take away the Bible and all its influences from our institutions, and expect that these will be preserved from decay. He that does not see, and will not acknowledge the power of the Bible in building up the whole framework of American institutions, is either unwise or insincere.

## X.

### By Lord Brougham. — Born 1788–1868.

*From a Speech in the House of Lords, December, 1837.*

THAT there should be no exclusion of *religious* instruction, but that, on the contrary, there should be a direct recognition of it, is my very decided opinion. I certainly am one of those who think that the bill should contain, in positive and express terms, a provision, that in all schools founded, extended, or improved, under this bill, the Scriptures shall be read. When I say that the Scriptures are one of the books which should be read in the schools, I, of course, mean that it should not be the only book read there: far from it; God forbid! — for the sake of religion and the Bible itself, God forbid! — but that, as a part of the reading in such schools, the Holy Scriptures should be used, with a proviso, of course, that any children of Jewish or Roman-Catholic parents attending such schools shall not be required to be present when the authorized version is read, unless the parent shall desire it.

## XI.

### From The Princeton Review.

*On Excluding the Religion of the Bible from Schools.*

THE separation of religion from secular education is not only impracticable, it is positively evil. The choice is not between religion and no religion, but between religion and irreligion, between Christianity and infidelity. The mere negative of Theism is Atheism. The absence of knowledge and faith in Christianity is infidelity. Even Byron had soul enough to make Lucifer say, —

> "He that bows not to God hath bowed to me."

As in a field, if you do not sow grain you will have weeds; so in the human mind, if you do not sow truth, you will have error. The attempt, therefore, to exclude religion from our common schools is an attempt to bring up in infidelity and atheism all that part of our population who depend on these schools for their education.

## XII.

### By Hon. Daniel Webster.

*On withholding Christian Instruction from the Young till they can judge for themselves.*

IT is vain to talk about the destructive tendency of such a system: to argue upon it is to insult the understanding of every man; *it is mere, sheer, low, ribald, vulgar deism and infidelity.* It opposes all that is in heaven, and all that is on earth that is worth being on earth. It destroys the connecting link between the creature and the Creator; it opposes that great system of universal benevolence and goodness that binds man to his Maker.

## XIII.

### By Karl Von Raumer (Germany).

*The Bible Intelligible to Children.*

IT should not be said that the children do not understand the Bible. The child has one understanding, and the man another, just as the artist has one very different from that of the learned commentator; and still Palestrina and Handel understood the fifty-third chapter of Isaiah better than Gesenius.

Poetic power should not be weakened by prosaic exposition. The whole modern phase of pedagogy has, among other characteristics, that of not merely neglecting, but by evil arts of destroying, the most active faculty of youth, — *a sensitive imagination.* This creative power of unreflecting simplicity, and the religious blessing which springs from that simplicity, are unknown to the dry pedagogues, who, by means of an intelligent torture of the understanding, which anticipates the period of mental maturity, would screw up the child to their much-praised "consciousness," and to the comprehension of every thing in general and in particular.

## XIV.

By Hon. JOHN COTTON SMITH, formerly President of the American Bible Society.

*On "Religious Instruction in our Public Schools."*

WE must restore the Bible to the schools. Who can tell how much of the delinquency which stains our judicial records may be attributed to ignorance of its divine precepts and sanctions? Who can estimate the number of thoughtless parents, — a number fearfully increased by the exclusion already mentioned, — who neglect or refuse to impress upon their children the duty of attentively reading the Bible? Establish it as an exercise in the common schools, and you make every child and youth in the Republic acquainted, of course, with a book, which, of all others, it behoves them to know, — a book whose divine origin, if there were no other proof, is demonstrated by its perfect adaption to every capacity, the humblest and the highest, to the condition of man through every stage and vicissitude of his earthly existence, as well as to his immortal destiny. Who can withhold such a book from the children of our country, and be blameless?

"Oh! come, let us walk in the light of the Lord,
As it beams from the page of His life-giving Word:
'Tis a lamp to our feet; and we go not astray
While we follow the path that's illumed by its ray, —
That path by the prophets and patriarchs trod,
Still bright with the steps of the chosen of God."

W. H. Burleigh.

## XV.

### By Hon. THOMAS S. GRIMKÉ. — 1786–1834.

*The Study of the Bible Essential to a Good Education.*

BUT has not the time come when a change may be advantageously and properly made? Is it credible that no change ever will be made,—that the Bible never will be an inseparable part of education, from the earliest and the lowest, to the latest and the highest? For myself, I have no doubt as to the answer to be given; and believing as I do, that one of the first duties of the Reformation was to have incorporated the Bible into the whole course of instruction, I trust that the time is not far distant when this principle will be universally acknowledged and acted on, "*that the Bible is the only good basis, and the only safe, enduring cement, of education.*"

## XVI.

### By Rev. JAMES W. ALEXANDER, D.D.—1804–1859.

*The Bible the Best Educator.*

HOLD up the great truth, that the Bible is the book to educate the age. Why not have it the chief thing in the family, in the school, in the academy, in the university? This day is *coming;* and, if you and I can introduce the *minutest corner* of the *wedge,* we shall be benefactors of our race. I can please and interest a child from the Bible. I can teach logic, ethics, rhetoric, and salvation from the Bible. May we not have a Bible-school? Sow the seed of the Word meekly, prayerfully: it must grow. The Bible, the Bible! it is this that must save America.

"How precious is the book divine,
By inspiration given!
Bright as a lamp its doctrines shine,
To guide our souls to heaven.
This lamp through all the tedious night
Of life shall guide our way,
Till we behold the clearer light
Of an eternal day."

Rev. JOHN FAWCETT.—1739–1817.

www.ingramcontent.com/pod-product-compliance
Lightning Source LLC
LaVergne TN
LVHW021419110826
845150LV00007B/1994

* 9 7 8 1 4 2 5 5 0 9 4 0 8 *